A Haphazard Miscellany of Poetry

Amber Sally Rose

BookLeaf
Publishing

India | USA | UK

Presentation by *BookLeaf Publishing*

Web: www.bookleafpub.com

E-mail: info@bookleafpub.com

ISBN: 9789357444613

First edition 2022

DEDICATION

I dedicate this collection of poetry to my amazing mother, Susan. The woman who raised me and my two siblings all on her own. I love you Mum, thank you for never giving up on me and for always supporting my dreams.

I'd also be remiss if I didn't acknowledge my namesake, my auntie Sally Rose. Love you loads xxx

ACKNOWLEDGEMENT

I would like to acknowledge all the people who made this book possible. My secondary school friend, Louisa, who's as much as a book nerd as me and is the person who ignited my love for writing. All the teachers who have helped me on my journey through the world of English writing. I'd also like to specially thank my poetry specialist university teachers; Emily Critchley who reawakened my passion for poetry and Dr. Cherry Smyth who continues to teach me new ways to understand and create poetry. Of course, I additionally have to thank BookLeaf Publishing without whom I never would have had the opportunity to publish this book.

PREFACE

I'm in a bunch of group chats (for university students) and someone sent an image about the #TheWriteAngle and after reading up on it, I thought this would be an amazing opportunity to share my poetry with people who aren't in my Advanced Poetry class. So I present to you my first poetry collection containing a number of poems that I thought were good enough to share with the public. Though please remember that I AM still in the process of learning how to write poetry well, so if they aren't that good just keep that in mind.

A Birthday Surprise

I knew we were in trouble when she walked into
the kitchen,
Where my brother and I were just trying to pitch
in.
Covered in flour, we looked up at her,
Tears welled up in our eyes, causing our vision
to blur.
"We just wanted to help, we never meant to
make a mess!",
My sibling and I cried out, our voices rising in
distress.

I knew we were in trouble when she angrily
ushered us out,
I still cried, but my brother began to pout.
"She never listens to us" He moaned,
"So it seems like our birthday surprise will have
to be postponed".
I wiped away my tears and smiled at my brother,
"You're right! You're right! We'll have to try
and bake another!"

I knew we were in trouble when she walked in
on us once more,
She looked at the flour, covering the floor.

Again she shouted, frustrated with us,
I remember thinking to myself; I wonder if she
understood our goal, would she make such a
fuss?
We sat in our room, debating over what to do,
Then an idea came to us, we knew just what to
do. We looked at each other and nodded, this
was our breakthrough.

I think we were in trouble when we heard the
front door open,
"Do you think she'll like it?"
"Here's hoping"
We picked up the decorated cupcakes and stood
in wait,
Her eyes widened when she set them upon the
plate.
The plate in question had 13 cupcakes on it,
"Look mum, we never quit!".
The mini cakes each had a single letter,
That spelt two words when you read them
together.

I knew we weren't in trouble when we saw her
face light up like the sun,
"Do you like it mum? Do you like what we've
done?".
Our mother smiled and nodded her head,
Then picked up an iced cupcake, covered in red.

"Is this what you were doing every day?,
When I came home and sent you away?".
"Yes mum, we wanted to surprise you. To thank
you for all the hard work you do,
You're our only parent and we wanted you to
enjoy your birthday, just like you used to"

I knew we weren't in trouble when our mother
pulled us in,
She gave us a tight hug and looked down at us
with a grin.
"I'm sorry for getting angry, I did not know,
"That you were trying to surprise me when you
were covered in dough".
We then took the cupcakes to the living room
and sang mum a birthday song,
Afterwards we danced and partied and enjoyed
ourselves all day long.

I knew we weren't in trouble because our mum
took us out for a surprise,
A movie, a movie, an enjoyment for our eyes.
After the movie, we went out for food,
We had McDonald's, what a delight!
Then we drove home, our car headlights were
bright,
As they shone into the darkness of the night.

I knew we weren't in trouble when our mum
tucked us into bed,
She made sure to give us each a kiss on the
head.
My brother and I went to sleep with a happy
smile,
Understanding how something little could really
go the mile.

I knew we weren't in trouble because our mum
just didn't understand,
We showed that we cared for her and everything
went as planned.

I knew we weren't in trouble because our mum
loves us and we love her,
We knew that there was nothing that could make
this family tear.

Love is a very interesting thing

Love is a very interesting thing.
It's a state that can be expressed in a number of
ways.
Some people write and some people sing.
Love can ignite us with a blaze
Or make us feel like we're soaring on wings.
Love can make us go crazy or simply amaze us.
We can love many things because of the
happiness they bring.
Love can be all-encompassing or it can just be a
phase.
Love can make you feel every day is spring,
Love can make you feel you're stuck in a maze,
As I mentioned before, love is a very interesting
thing.
It can be expressed in a number of ways.
It can make us cry and it can make us shout,
Some might say that's what love's all about.

Death Is Coming

We dread it coming but we know it to be true,
No one can escape it; not me nor you.
Death is coming, it's nothing new.

All life much eventually come to an end.
We only have a moment to make our debut,
Truly, our time on this Earth is hard to
comprehend.

We dread it coming but we know it to be true.
To suddenly stop existing must be unnerving
and what makes it worse are the people we leave
behind.

Imagining the deaths of those we love,
The end of their lives takes a piece of them with
you
and there's nothing about that we can do.

What will happen when you're gone?
Will people care so much that they can't forge
ahead?
Or will they care so little that they easily move
on instead?

We dread it coming but we know it to be true.
Just like living, dying is a part of nature,
And just like birth, your death allows you to
"live" anew.
Death is coming, it's nothing new.

Nature's Majesty

They teach you about nature from a textbook,
but really what can you learn from that?
You only need to know where to look
to learn the beauty of humanity's habitat.

Look up
and you'll find the sky.
A boundless blanket of blue
stretching high and far above you.
Fluffs of white float past your eyes,
the sky's cotton candy that can never crystalize.

 Look down,
and you'll notice the earth.
Covered in green grass
that has been flattened beneath the many steps
taken upon it.
Ahead a rabbit pops its head out the ground.
The small creature looks about before coming
out of the ground,
and as expected starts to hop around.

Look around,
and if you're lucky you'll see a tree or two.

Grand brown trunks holding up a bounteous
foliage
that come in a variety of shapes and hues,
and in the right season you may even see pink or
white too.

Man has created many things.
They can even fly without wings.
Man has created many things
that are capable of pulling one's heartstrings.

Man has truly created many things,
in their attempts to make the world a prettier
place.
They try and try but here's the thing:
They can never outdo the planet's natural grace.
The majesty of nature will always outshine the
human race.

Words, that's all they are

Words.
A concept.
A language device.
Things we use to communicate.
That's all they are.
Yet they hold this mysterious power,
to make us feel or act in certain ways
that are sometimes hard to explain.

I love you.
Three simple words,
that's all they are.
Yet it could be said that these words are three of
the most powerful in the English language.
These words can make us cry.
They can make us sing.
They can make us feel a number of things.

Words…
That's all they are.
An element of language

that can be both meaningful and meaningless.
They can be paired with others or used alone,
to convey or make our feelings known.

I hate you.
Three simple words.
That's all they are.
So why can these words cause our hearts to
break?
Why does the impact of these words feel akin to
a bullet?
Why are these words capable of causing so
much hurt?
These three little words that are so short, so curt.

Words.
That's all they are.
Only a concept.
Only a language device.
Only a thing we use to communicate.
Only an element of language.
That's all they are…

…aren't they?

Social Butterfly

They used to be a social butterfly.
They were rarely seen at home
but ever since the lockdown
They've become trapped.

A social butterfly with no space to spread its
wings.
A social butterfly deprived of the one thing it
needs.
There are days when the butterfly will only lay
in bed
feeling as if their wings have been clipped.
Their mind tells them to get up
but at the same time, it asks: "What is the
point?"

And so the butterfly stays in its room.
Curtains drawn to hide their antisocial shame.
Then all of a sudden, the butterfly hears a ring.

One ring…

…Two rings…

…Three rings.

They look up and see a familiar face,
illuminated on the screen of their phone.
They grab their phone but hesitate.
Afraid they've forgotten how to be the butterfly
they once were.

The ringing stops and a voice message starts to
play.
This voice reminds the butterfly that they're not
alone
and suddenly their world doesn't seem so grey.
They finally get out of bed,
knowing they're not an antisocial butterfly.
They may never be the butterfly they once were
but they can now learn a new way to be a social
butterfly.

Cannot, Do not, Must not stop

Rushing forward.
Panting.
Heaving.
Lungs feeling empty.
Catching my breath was a dream
because I could not stop.

Cannot stop.
Do not stop.
I am unable to stop,
no matter what.

Sweat secreting.
Cascading.
Rolling.
Coating my body.
Stopping to wipe the moisture away was a
fantasy
because I could not stop.

Cannot stop.
Do not stop.

I am unable to stop,
no matter what.

Limbs hurting.
Aching.
Throbbing.
Screaming at me to stop,
yet they knew I could not.

Cannot stop.
Do not stop.
I am unable to stop,
no matter what.

Heart beating.
Thumping.
Pounding.
Swiftly pumping blood so my body would not
stop
because my mind knew my body could not stop.

Cannot stop.
Do not stop.
I am unable to stop,
no matter what.

Why couldn't I stop? I don't know.

DO NOT STOP.

I just knew that something bad would happen if I
did.

CANNOT STOP.

What would happen? I do not know.

I AM UNABLE TO STOP, NO MATTER
WHAT.

My mind is a jumbled mess
but this one fact stays clear in my mind:
I must keep running because I cannot stop.

DO NOT STOP.

I keep running,
trusting my mind and repeating its mantra:

Cannot stop.
Do not stop.
I am unable to stop, no matter what.

No matter what I must not stop.

Space - A canvas

Space.
A giant black canvas,
spattered with colours of all different kinds.
From the blues and yellows of the Milky Way
galaxy.
To the sandy tones of planet Jupiter.

Space.
A canvas that's forever expanding,
adding more and more to its giant black canvas.
Like places that rain diamonds by the tonne,
or stars that burn far hotter than our sun.

Space.
A truly wonderous work of art
with rock things and planet rings.
With black holes and amazing light shows.
A never-ending void our planet calls home.

My Love

I smile contentedly,
Wrapped up in my blankets.
My head rests upon my fluffy pillow.
My body lies upon my love.
The contact between us comforting my very
soul.

My lover's embrace fills my heart with warmth.
A sense of safety stretching and enveloping me,
No harm can come to me while we are together.

Rays of sunlight peak through my curtains,
I groan, sinking deeper into my cocoon of
blankets.
I won't let the sun separate my love and me.

Outside, the sound of birds singing starts.
My love tries to comfort me as I toss and turn.
To me the birds' singing was anything but sweet.
I push my face into my pillow to drown out the
noise.
I won't let the break of dawn separate my love
and me.

The cacophony of engines and horns outside
slowly grows louder.
The universe is working against me and my
love,
doing everything it can to separate us.
But I won't let it achieve its goal.

I manage to block out the noise,
I manage to stay close to my love,
I manage to enjoy the time we spend together,
I manage-BEEP BEEP BEEP

I sigh loudly, infuriated by this sound I cannot
ignore.
Picking up the source of the infernal racket, I
swiftly silence it.
I reluctantly rise from my blankets,
Knowing it was time to get myself ready.
I know it was only a delusion,
wishing that I could stay with my love forever.

I get out of bed, sad to part from it
and set my laptop up for another day of Teams.

What is treasure?

Treasure, treasure, treasure you say?
Treasure, treasure, where does it lay?
Well, first I think we should address this…
What do YOU think treasure is?

Is treasure something shiny?
Something that has value?
Like a sunken chest filled with gold,
That has to be at least a couple of centuries old

Treasure, treasure, you're still here?
Then I suppose you think that treasure lies
elsewhere?
Perhaps not in a chest, but somewhere close,
Let me just go take a peek at my notes

Ah, yes. How about this?
Is treasure something that fills you with bliss?
Like a perfect day where nothing's amiss,
Or perhaps, if you're old enough, treasure to you
could be true love's kiss

Treasure, treasure, still you stay?
It's good to see you can't be swayed.

If you still have not found your answer to my
question,
Might I be so polite as to offer a suggestion?
Look not with your eyes, but with your heart,
because to find the answer you must be truly
smart.
Be sure to keep that in mind, otherwise you may
become blind,
To the answer you may very well have to find.

Is treasure maybe something intangible?
Something one may consider unchangeable?
Like a mother's love for her child,
Or a relationship that against all odds prevailed

Treasure, treasure, perhaps it's time,
That I stop fooling around like a mime,
And tell you what I think treasure to be,
Though I suspect you already know the answer,
to some degree.
Or maybe you don't, I guess we'll just have to
see.

Treasure, treasure, what is treasure?
Treasure can be a mix of all the things above,
Treasure can be there for you when push comes
to shove.
Treasure can be shiny,
Treasure can be dull,

Treasure can be anything, just anything you
know,
As long as it's special to whoever possesses it.

Treasure can be a million things to someone
with wit,
Treasure can be a single thing to someone if it so
befits.
Treasure can be an invisible thing to those it's
important to,
As we've so seen a verse ago or two.

So…
What is treasure?
There are many answers to this question,
But perhaps the answer that matters most,
Is that treasure is something you hold close,
Something you cherish and love.

Magnificent
Waterfall

The sound of rushing water reaches my ears.
I find myself drawn to the noise,
much akin to a moth drawn to a flame.

I grow closer, my anticipation rising
as the sound grows louder and louder.
My imagination runs wild.
Visualising what I'm about to see.
Will it be a lake?
Or maybe a stream?

The sound is ever so loud now.
I run around the corner and look down.
I see a river running in front of me.
It murmurs while it passes over the rocks on the
riverbed.

The sunlight creates a spotlight.
As if urging me to look where it shone.
I follow the beam of light and stand there in
shock.
My imagination couldn't begin to comprehend

the splendour of this sight.

A beauteous waterfall,
towering high above me.
The waterfall colliding with the river
is what created that oh so soothing sound.

The natural beauty of the world causes me to
falter.
I watch the sparkling water cascade downward,
hoping I never forget this moment.
This moment where I first
laid my eyes upon a magnificent waterfall.

If we were together

We can never be together.
I know this to be true,
yet I can't help but wonder
what it would be like if I was with you.

Would you caress my hair like you do with her?
Or would you pat my head to tell me you love
me?
If I asked you to hold my hand would you do it
with care?
Or would you only grab my hand to keep me
safe from strangers?

I watch how you act with her
and jealously burns in my heart.
I get excited when she leaves
because then it's just you and me.
But then she comes back and again,
the green-eyed monster inside me rages to life.

If I told you her secrets would you still like her
then?
If you knew the true intensity of my feelings
would you accept them?
Or would you just laugh and brush them off?

There are so many ways I imagine our love
blossoming.
Too many ways to count
but none of these ways will ever come true
until I am the only one who's after you.

Seasonal Transition

The sun's rays illuminate the Earth,
While the air turns crisp and cool,
Now you know autumn is upon you.

Fragility

The fragility
Of nature is revealed here
As gravity forces the leaves downwards.

The Golden Hues of Falling Leaves

The season has changed.
Golden hues paint the landscape
and flicker through the clouds.
Fallen leaves rustle underfoot,
as the kids jump around.
Nature heralds all.

Autumnal Equinox

The equinox has arrived,
Equalising autumn day
and night.

Family Promises

"Promise. A noun: A declaration or assurance
that one will do something or that a particular
thing will happen"

My sister.
A little girl full of wonder.
She continues to be curious,
even though it often makes our mum furious.
A little girl that I will forever adore.
This is a promise that I will forever store
within my heart forevermore.

My brother.
A young man who doubles as a gamer.
He may be antisocial, but that won't change my
feelings.
My love for him is as high as castle ceilings.
I'll never stop loving him with all my heart.
This is my promise to my brother who's hella
smart.

My mother.
A proud woman who can fight her own battles,
as well as the battles of her three loving kids.
She's strong and hardly ever wrong.

I know with her I'll always belong.
I love my mum for everything she's done.
I promise to love my mum with everything I've
got
because with her I've won the single parent
jackpot.

Me, Myself and Why

There are many things that make me me; my DNA, my memories and my upbringing are three very important factors. But we mustn't forget the things that I am in control of that make me who I am. My likes and dislikes, my favourite things-Now you may say that these cannot really tell you who I am as they are susceptible to change. To that I say nay! You are wrong! These may change, but whenever they change, they reveal another aspect of myself to you.

Let's start at the beginning, shall we? Colours are everywhere and are beautiful-to all those lucky enough to see them-Can you remember the first colour you saw? The first colour present in your earliest memory? Because I sure can't! I remember there being a multitude of colours, but if you asked me to name those colours I'd be stumped because I can't really remember what all those colours actually were.

Now if you ask me to remember what my favourite food is, that I could do-especially since I had it for dinner today. I'm a pizza loving girl! You can eat from point to crust or crust to point; you can leave the crust or eat the toppings turning your pizza into a plain one. You can even roll it up and stuff it into your mouth if you want to be done quickly.

I couldn't talk about me, myself and why without mentioning my family. I'm a weird individual, you wanna know why? Because my family are a bunch of weirdos, there's just no other way to put it. They find laughter in the silliest of circumstances. When I was younger and could barely speak, there was a certain word my uncle loved to hear me say. The word in question was "suck". Seems simple enough to pronounce, yet my young mouth couldn't form the word. It did, however, form another word. A word ending in -uck and beginning with I think you know what.

I don't like thinking about this, but it's also a part of me. I fear that I'm going to fail my studies. I fear that I won't achieve my dream job. Though these pale in comparison to my biggest fear, which is the fear of letting my family down. Let's think about noises now. These are also all around us and can be beautiful or annoying-again to those who are able to hear them. I've found that I don't much like the sound of a busy road, it unsettles me for reasons I do not yet know. To me, a beautiful sound is that of a violin. No matter what I'm doing or how I'm feeling, a violin always manages to sound so appealing. Especially if it's being played by Lindsey Stirling.

As a flower blooms and brings us happiness with its beautiful petals, I wish I will someday be able to bring beauty and happiness into this world with my own two hands. This may all seem random to you, but to me this piece has meaning. And so, I leave you with this question: What do you believe is the true meaning of random.

www.ingramcontent.com/pod-product-compliance
Lightning Source LLC
LaVergne TN
LVHW021314200726
843509LV00012B/1922